WE CAN DEAL WITH BULLYING!

I dedicate this book to family and friends, lifelong and new.

And an overdue huge thank you to Jim and to Alex for the generous gift of your time, invaluable suggestions, eagle eyes and honest critique of each book in progress. The results are far better than I would ever have achieved without you.

Gina

WE CAN DEAL WITH BULLYING!

EMPOWERMENT FOR YOUNG PEOPLE

GINA DAWSON
ILLUSTRATED BY KATE BOUMAN

NEW
HOLLAND

CONTENTS

GET THE FACTS

Have you ever been bullied?

Do you know someone who has? You probably do, because bullying is way more common than many people think. If you are being bullied I want you to remember that you are never alone, even though it may feel that way. There are lots of people who understand how awful being bullied feels, and many of them will want to help you if you ask them.

Talking about bullying can be hard. You may feel scared, hurt, embarrassed, upset, confused or all sorts of emotions. In fact, some people become so confused, they begin thinking there's something wrong with them, or that they are in some way to blame for being bullied. That's never true. It's **NEVER** your fault. It's just that being bullied can make you feel really bad!

You might think you should try to cope with bullying yourself. Maybe you're worried that if you speak up it will make things worse or you won't be believed. But as hard as it can be, it's important to speak up about bullying, because it can help you – and other people too.

Nobody is all good or all bad. We can all be really nice, really nasty and everything in between. But remember, we **CHOOSE** how we behave.

So when we understand why a person chooses to **bully**, we begin to feel **EMPOWERED**. That means we feel stronger. And that feels a bit better.

This book aims to help you remain healthy, in control and feeling positive about yourself, regardless of what a **bully** may say or do. And that feels fantastic!

Read this book alone or with an adult or a friend, and share what you learn.

Working together and helping each other is really important in our stand against bullying.

If you're bullied and you can't sort it out quickly, do your best to tell at least three people clearly and accurately what is happening. Tell them how you feel and ask for their help. Examples of people to tell are:

- An adult in charge - like your teacher, group leader or coach.

- Your parent or an adult you live with.

- A trustworthy friend, or an older brother or sister.

Talking about bullying is **NOT** telling tales. Talking to people you trust will mean you feel less alone, and each of these people can give you a different kind of support and help you to decide what to do next.

Never remain silent. Talking helps you ~ and may help others too.

Now, let's take a look at ...

WHAT IS BULLYING?

The word 'bullying' is sometimes used when it isn't really bullying at all. If someone argues with you, ignores you, thoughtlessly upsets you or says something mean, you may feel angry, hurt, sad or worried. But it's a fact that we can all be unthoughtful or hurtful at times, sometimes without meaning to.

Bullying is when someone deliberately sets out to make you feel ashamed, afraid or upset over and over again. If they succeed at doing that, the **bully** feels good, and they'll probably keep it up.

Bullying can be physical, where the **bully** tries to hurt you or damage your property. It can be verbal and include insults, threats or nasty remarks about you. It may involve excluding you from a group or spreading rumours about you. Then there is cyberbullying – a particularly cowardly type of bullying where the **bully** uses phones, emails or social media to spread their nasty words or images.

Any type of bullying can be very upsetting, and it may feel like it will never end. Your feelings, confidence and self-esteem can be seriously damaged.

Bullying is NOT a joke and is NEVER okay.

It's important to know that although you can't control what a **bully** does, you **CAN** control how you react to it. And that one thing can make a **HUGE** difference!

You can decide if you are going to be ...

A VICTIM OR A TARGET

Some people may say you are a victim if you're bullied. While that is true, the problem is that one of the meanings of the word 'victim' is someone who feels helpless, and that there's nothing they can do to change things. That's not true and it's also a sad and sometimes dangerous way to think.

So instead, I'll say that a person being bullied is a **TARGET**. The **bully** wants to hurt their **target** by hitting them with their words or actions. But a **target** can learn to make themselves harder to hit. If the **bully** keeps missing their **target**, or isn't sure if they hit it or not, bullying stops being fun. Then they may stop, or try to find someone who is more fun to **bully**.

So this is really important ...

- Don't become a helpless victim.
- Be a **target** who can make choices and feel empowered.

Always follow your school **BULLYING POLICY** and encourage your friends to as well. But that can only work if you're bullied at school.

And the fact is ...

BULLYING CAN HAPPEN ANYWHERE!

Bullying can happen anywhere that people communicate, so that includes classrooms, school yards, on the street, at sport, public transport, at camp, shops, clubs, on social media, in homes – in fact anywhere at all!

Bullies want to feel safe so they usually choose places where they believe their target won't be a threat to them. Sometimes they **bully** when there are people about, which also gives them an opportunity to show off and get attention. Cowardly bullies operate from a distance using devices.

Being bullied at your age is tough. You're growing up, trying to sort stuff out, and you want to have friends and fit in. That's why it's important to protect your feelings and self-esteem and deal with bullying wherever and however it happens.

Bullies can be males or females of any age, from all sorts of backgrounds and any shape or size. In other words they look just like everyone else! That's because anyone can choose to **bully**, so it's a good idea for each of us to ask ourselves honestly sometimes ...

Would anyone think the way I am behaving is bullying?

Be honest with yourself, as we all have room to improve on the way we behave towards other people at times. That's something to think about, but in the meantime let's get empowered! If you are bullied:

- Never hide away, even though you feel like it. It just makes things worse.

- Keep doing things you usually do, even when it feels hard.

- If you feel unsafe, ask a friend, family member or someone you know if you can stay near them so you're not alone.

- Keep talking and asking for support.

You may be surprised to know that ...

NO ONE LIKES A BULLY!

It's true! The target certainly doesn't, but nor do the kids who know about the bullying or even those who hang out with the **bully**.

Okay, so maybe you're thinking that's hard to believe, because if people didn't like a **bully** they wouldn't hang out with them, or they'd do something to stop them.

It's not that simple because although it might seem like they approve or don't care, often they don't approve and they **DO** care a lot.

And to top it off, often bullies don't like themselves! Not even the tough, smart or popular ones, because deep down they know the reason they are behaving the way they are and they wish they weren't.

So let's talk about ...

SOME OF THE REASONS PEOPLE CHOOSE TO BULLY

Bullies may look tough, confident and successful, but often that's not how they feel. Think about it. If a person feels good about themselves, why would they take time out from their happy life to **bully** someone? They wouldn't!

Many bullies have loads of problems. Some feel miserable, scared, insecure or angry. Okay, not all bullies. A few people are just plain

mean or think bullying is fun, but every **bully** has something to prove to themselves or someone else.

You may know bullies and find this hard to believe. So let's look deep into the mind of a **bully**. We may find someone who ...

- Feels weak so they **bully** to prove they are powerful and strong.

- Feels lousy, so they **bully** to prove that they can make someone else feel worse than they do.

- Is desperate to be popular, so they **bully** to prove they are clever or entertaining.

- Is afraid that their target is more popular, interesting, smarter or successful than they are. By excluding them or destroying their reputation they get rid of the competition.

- Is lonely, so they **bully** to prove they don't care that they have no friends, when really they care a lot.

- Is angry, so they **bully** to get revenge.

- Is frightened or ashamed. Sadly they may have been bullied themselves so they cover it up and feel safer by bullying others.

I could keep going but you get my point. Bullying is often just one big cover-up for someone who needs to prove something to themselves and everyone else.

So the **bully's** secret is out! We could almost feel sorry for them — but not quite because bullying can cause a lot of harm.

So ...

- Be the one to raise the topic of bullying with friends and classmates.

- Ask your teacher to support class discussions.

The more we talk, the more we understand what makes bullies tick, and the easier it is to stand together against bullying!

When a **bully** sees we aren't impressed or scared, they'll know that they aren't proving anything. They even start to look a bit silly.

That's when the bully begins to lose power.

It won't happen instantly. In fact, to begin with they may get even more desperate, nasty or angry. They may try harder or use different tactics. If that doesn't work, they may stop bullying altogether or perhaps go looking for an easier target.

And that's why ...

ANYONE CAN BE A TARGET!

If you are a target, it isn't because there's something wrong with you, or even because you **ARE** you. It isn't personal.

If you moved house tomorrow, a new target would take your place. It doesn't matter **WHO** the target is, so long as the **bully** has one.

You are a random target.

It's NOT about you!

So remember – don't be a helpless victim. Think like a target and see the **bully** for what they are – someone with something to prove.

Say aloud and silently to yourself as often as you can ...

- 'There is nothing about me that makes me deserve to be bullied.'

- 'Just because the **bully** says it, it doesn't make it true.'

BELIEVE these words! They are true even though your brain may try to trick you into thinking that they're not.

Anyone can be a target but because bullies don't want to think too hard, often they'll choose targets they think will be easy.

Bullies may **target** someone of a different culture, religion, skin colour, sexual orientation, body size or shape, style of dressing, disability or simply someone who looks or sounds different. That's because it is easier to find put-downs and nasty insults to hurt them.

Never change who you are or how you look to suit the **bully**. It doesn't work and may even make things worse.

Everyone understands that being a **target** is painful.

So the next thing to understand is ...

BULLIES NEED A REACTION TO FEEL GOOD

Without a reaction, the **bully** isn't proving how tough, clever or popular they are. But if they get a reaction it encourages them to do it again.

If the **target** shows they are upset, angry or ashamed, hides away or gives in to the **bully's** demands, the **bully** feels strong, powerful and in control. They may even think that it proves just how good they are.

Adults may have told you to simply ignore the **bully.** That's good advice, but it isn't always simple. That's because 'ignore' can mean not to care, pretend it isn't happening or take no notice.

But of course you care and it **IS** happening! Never ignore painful feelings and emotions, because that can make you ill or stressed.

So instead of saying 'ignore' let's say you can **CONTROL** how you respond to bullying, by:

- Trying to show no reaction.

- Accepting that you feel hurt inside, but showing a cool front on the outside.

Even though on the inside you are reacting by feeling upset or scared, the **bully** can't see that, so they don't know if their bullying is working or not.

So ...

- Appear calm and unfussed.

- Stand tall, with your head high and mouth closed.

- It is usually best to avoid eye contact.

- Don't hang around. Calmly walk towards somewhere safe.

If you can manage that, the **bully** won't have proven anything, so you'll have done really well.

It isn't always easy to **NOT** show a reaction, but do your best. Try blocking out the **bully's** words with brain tricks, such as ...

- Concentrate hard on where you're headed.

- Count inside your head.

- Imagine the **bully** looking ridiculous.

- Imagine a clear protective shield that bounces the **bully's** words back.

- Rehearse something in your head, like a speech or a song.

Try different things and do what works for you. If you need help coping, there are trained adults who help people learn how to remain calm and in control. Ask for help.

Tell friends what is happening and ask them to support you by sticking close, following your lead and behaving in the same way you do. You can even keep chatting, as if you aren't interested in what the **bully** is saying.

Having support makes it easier to cope. Talk about bullying and ways to deal with it. You can even try role-play, alone or with a friend, so you have a plan of exactly what you'll do if it happens.

The **bully** won't be happy if they don't get a reaction – but that's their problem! If you keep it up, chances are they'll move onto another **target** or better still, stop altogether.

If they don't stop bullying, think about ...

A FRIENDLY TALK WITH THE BULLY

Okay, each situation is different so you need to think through what you are going to do next. If you can, share your ideas with someone you trust so they can support you.

One idea is to think about talking to the **bully**. You could do that at the time the bullying is happening, or you could do it afterwards.

If you choose to speak when the bullying is happening ...

- Try not to show you feel angry or upset.

- Smile so you appear calm and unfussed.

- If their comment is based on truth, say something like 'You could be right!'

- If the comment is false, say something like 'That's your opinion!' or 'You can't be serious!'

- Using sarcasm sometimes works, with comments like 'Hey, why didn't I think of that!' in a friendly voice.

These ways of responding are called 'fogging' because the **bully** doesn't know if their insults have affected you or not.

Keep walking – wave if you like – and don't argue or give them an opportunity to show off.

If you decide that you want to try talking to the **bully** privately ...

- Always tell a trusted person what you plan to do, when and where.

- Never do this if you feel unsafe.

- Plan ahead so you know what you are going to say.

It's a good idea to rehearse using 'I' statements. These are statements that begin with the word 'I', such as 'I feel ...' or 'I would like to know ...'

When you feel ready, ask the **bully** if you can meet with them and if they agree ...

- Choose a place that's neutral, like a park bench or café with people around.
- Put on your calm look and start with a positive statement like 'Thanks for coming'.
- Ask them if you've done something to upset them, or why they are targeting you.
- Listen to their answers and don't interrupt.
- Try to come to an agreement, even if that is simply to stay away from each other.
- Remember, your aim is to end the bullying so pleading, shouting or threatening won't help.

If the **bully** shouts, wait until they've finished, and answer calmly. They'll probably be surprised you didn't shout back and lower their voice.

Be firm but don't argue and never use their nasty methods, because that just gives them more weapons to use against you.

Sometimes talking to the **bully** works and sometimes it doesn't, but either way, afterwards you'll know where you stand.

- You can only do your best.
- Be proud of yourself for trying, even if it didn't work.
- Make sure you keep your trusted adults and friends informed about where you are and what you are doing to deal with the bullying.

Sadly some bullies won't stop, so you may want to try ...

TALKING FIRMLY TO THE BULLY

You can speak firmly to the **bully** while the bullying is happening or soon afterwards.

Again, if possible, plan ahead and remember that you want to end the bullying, not score points. It's tempting to want to prove to the **bully** that you are right and they are wrong, or that you are smarter than they are, but remind yourself that will get you nowhere and anyway, it's not the reason you are there. You are there because you want the bullying to end. It's best to talk firmly when there are people around, so don't set up a private meeting for this. Make sure you are in a safe place and have support.

- Rehearse what you are going to say, try to remain calm and take a deep breath before you begin.

- Make eye contact and use a firm voice.

- Raise your voice a bit so you sound serious but never shout.

- Tell the **bully** to stop doing what they are doing immediately.

- Use 'I' statements.

- Empty threats never work – so don't say anything you don't intend to do.

Once you have delivered your message, look for a reaction:

- If the **bully** seems to be taking notice or being reasonable, more talking may help.

- If they walk away saying nothing, let them go and wait to see if the bullying stops.

- If they say they won't stop, clearly tell them the consequences of continuing, including that you will report them.

- If they become hostile or angry, leave the scene immediately – and report it.

Remember ...

- Always put your safety first before deciding whether to talk to the **bully**.

- If nothing changes, take the action you said you would take.

Now, there's usually more to this picture than the target and the **bully**.

So it's time we take a look at ...

BYSTANDERS

Bystanders are people who see or know about bullying but don't do anything to stop it. Some may even laugh or encourage the **bully**. Even if **bystanders** just watch and say nothing, the **bully** feels popular, smart or funny.

If you've been bullied, you'll know how much you wished a **bystander** would help you. But remember, most **bystanders** aren't enjoying watching the bullying either, even though it may not look that way. Knowing this may help you remain calm and to not react.

If there's a friend amongst the **bystanders**:

- Try to make eye contact so they know you've seen them.

- Afterwards you could speak to them and ask for their support.

- Don't accuse a **bystander** or sound angry, because if you do they'll try to defend their actions.

- Tell them how you felt and ask if things might be different next time.

Anyone can be an accidental bystander.

Even you!

Imagine you are walking along the street with other kids. Someone is walking towards you and the next thing you know, someone in your group is bullying them. Suddenly you're a bystander, without wanting or meaning to be. And if everyone stands around watching, what will you do?

Maybe you'd like to do something to stop it, but that's not always easy. It's hard speaking up against people who seem popular or powerful. It's easier to blend in than stand out.

Perhaps you'll feel afraid that if you speak up, someone won't like it and you'll be out of the group or worse still, the next target. That's scary so maybe you'll stay quiet.

You may hate what you are seeing, but feel helpless to change anything, or even worry that defending the target may make things worse for them. Perhaps you will figure that if no one else is doing something there must be a reason.

Chances are you'll feel sorry for the target and maybe even upset. Although some bystanders think bullying is funny, most don't and will feel uncomfortable and relieved it isn't them.

You may even feel guilty for not helping, especially if the bullying is particularly nasty.

Bystanders can do a lot of damage. It's upsetting for the target to see people watching and doing nothing to help, while the bully gets attention and looks popular and cool. So if you find yourself being a bystander, you have choices to make.

It's important to stay safe, so never take action if it doesn't feel right.

Imagine if every bystander walked away! The bully wouldn't feel popular, smart or funny anymore and a lot of bullying would stop. What a great day that would be!

Every small step makes a difference to the way we battle bullying. Here are some steps bystanders can take:

- Quietly walk away. Don't support the **bully** by watching.

- If you are with a friend, speak quietly to them and ask them to walk with you.

- If you don't feel safe leaving, look down or look sympathetically at the target.

- With online bullying, never participate by 'liking' and never share or pass on posts or photos.

- Don't do anything that may be seen to show support for the **bully**.

Do the best you can. Even if you can't stop the bullying, feel proud you actively didn't support it.

If you are a bystander, there may be times when you can do something. That's great, because EVERY stand against bullying makes a difference!

- Talk with your friends about how to react if you become bystanders.

- Support each other. There's power and safety in numbers.

There are many ways to take a stand against bullying, so let's look at ...

WAYS TO BE AN UPSTANDER

Sometimes a bystander searches their feelings and decides to become an **upstander**. That means they decide to speak up for the target or try to help them in some other way.

Upstanders actively try to do something to stop bullying and that's why **upstanders** can really change things!

An **upstander** can make a big impression on the **bully**, **target** and **bystanders**. That's because when an **upstander** takes action ...

- The **bully** sees that they aren't looking so cool or clever.

- The **target** sees that someone cares and is trying to help.

- The **bystanders** who felt afraid to **Upstand** themselves may feel more confident following the **upstander's** lead.

If we were all upstanders, we could wipe out a lot of bullying.

If you decide to be an **upstander**, think carefully about what you are prepared to do. It can be tricky. You might worry about what will happen next, what others will think and whether there will be consequences. It's important you are safe, so never put yourself in danger.

While it's good to have a plan, chances are you may come across bullying and have to decide on the spot. If that happens you can only do your best, and don't beat yourself up afterwards if you didn't do what you hoped you would.

If you know about ongoing bullying, you can plan your **Upstand**. It's a good idea to ask friends if they will join you. It's safer, plus it sends a stronger message to the **bully**, **target** and **bystanders**.

So how can you and your friends be upstanders?

One **Upstanding** approach is to report bullying.

- Report it to a trusted adult or follow the **bullying policy** at your school or organisation.

- Provide as much information as you can but stick to facts.

- If you are nervous and want to be anonymous, let the person you report to know that.

- Ask friends to back up your report, or even better, report it as a group.

Reporting bullying is a positive thing to do so you should feel good about it. It is not telling tales.

Another **Upstanding** approach is to speak to the **bully**.

- Let the **target** know that you do not agree with the bullying and that you are going to tell the **bully** that.

- Find fellow **upstanders** who will come with you if you can.

- In a strong, firm voice, tell the **bully** clearly that the way they are behaving is wrong, and they must stop it.

- Calmly explain that if anything bad happens to the **target** the **bully** will be in serious trouble.

- If they don't agree, tell them you will report them. If they turn nasty or the bullying continues, do exactly that.

Another positive thing **upstanders** can do is raise awareness. The more people who understand why bullying is happening and who want to do something about it, the bigger effect it has.

- Talk to friends and people you know.

- Ask your teachers to have class discussions about safe ways to **upstand** against bullying.

And finally, you are an upstander if you ...

SUPPORT THE TARGET

Whether they are a friend or someone you don't know, think about how they may be feeling and how awful it would be to feel that way. Then work out how to show support.

If they seem alone, try to include them. Ask them if they'd like to sit with you, study together or whatever feels right. Tell them you don't agree with the bullying. Ask if they're okay and if there's anything you can do to help.

They might not want to talk about it, and that's okay. Don't pressure, as they may feel uncomfortable or afraid. You can still ask them to hang out sometimes and talk about other things.

If they refuse your offer, they will still know that you tried – and so will you. That's a good way to feel. Let them know you are ready to listen and help if they change their mind. Be available if that happens.

You could also talk to your friends about including the target in your group, or for different people to offer help. Feeling included can make all the difference to someone who is being bullied.

- Reach out to the target so they know someone cares.
- Encourage them to get help and support them as best you can.

The key to ending bullying is to Upstand together. In numbers we are safer and stronger!

If the target wants to talk about the bullying, don't interrupt. They may have so much fear and anger inside them that they just want to let it all out. Sometimes talking can help people decide what to do next ...

- Be sensitive.
- Listen quietly and respectfully.
- If they ask, try to make helpful suggestions about dealing with the problem.

- Share what you have learned about bullying from this book or other responsible places.

- Assure them that bullying is never their fault.

- Don't break their trust. If they talk to you, don't repeat what they said to other people.

- Show them they are not alone and that you and other people want to help.

- Keep checking how they are. Don't talk to them once and forget them.

- Get information. In many countries there are phone numbers where kids can talk to adults to get advice. Pass them on.

- Encourage the person to report the bullying. Offer to go with them if they don't want to go alone.

- If you are worried about their safety or mental health, you'll need to tell an adult what's happening.

- Explain to the target that you intend to do this because you care and are worried. Do it straight away before anything else happens.

- Look after yourself. If you feel unsafe trying to help or find the situation too upsetting, talk to an adult immediately.

Again you can only do your best. If you aren't able to help, be proud that you tried.

So ...

IF YOU ARE BEING BULLIED

I hope you now feel ...

- Less like a helpless victim and more like an empowered target.

- A bit more in control and a little less afraid.

- You can grow stronger and wiser because of what's happening.

And you ...

- Accept this is not your fault and you have done nothing to deserve it.

- Know there are people who will help if you ask.

- Feel more determined to do something about bullying.

Bullies use different tactics. You probably know most of them, and some bullies use several methods at once.

So let's take a look at different ways bullies work and how to deal with them. It's best if you read all the sections to get the big picture, but if you're being bullied and are in a hurry for some answers, jump to the headings that you think will help you first.

Let's start with ...

PHYSICAL BULLYING

If the **bully** tries to frighten or control you by physically hurting you or by stealing or damaging your property:

- **Plan ahead**. Avoid the **bully**. Ask friends to stay near you in places where you can't avoid them.

- **Act calm**. Try not to show fear. Ignore the **bully** and walk away. If they try to stop you, look them in the eye and say, 'Stop this' as firmly as you can.

- **Don't hang around.** Always put your safety first.
- **Don't physically fight back.** It may make the **bully** nastier or you could be blamed for starting the fight.
- **If in danger hand it over.** There is no item worth more than your safety, regardless of how expensive it is!
- **Shout** to attract attention, run fast and tell someone immediately.

THREATS AND BLACKMAIL

If the **bully** threatens, blackmails or tries to force you to do things you don't want to:

- **Work out** exactly what you are afraid of and why. That's important. It may be the threats or blackmail are harmless.
- **Never give in** to the **bully's** demands. They'll just get more demanding. They may carry out their threats anyway.
- **Refuse** to do anything that feels humiliating or wrong, even if the **bully** threatens something nasty if you don't.
- **Remember,** if you do what the **bully** says you may end up in trouble or humiliated.
- **Surprise** the **bully.** Act calm and pretend to ignore them.
- **Make a joke** about their demand or laugh as if it's really funny. They may be surprised that you don't seem to care or are having fun at their expense.
- **If you are afraid** and believe the threats or blackmail are serious you must stop it immediately. Confide in at least one adult quickly.
- **Tell the complete story.** For an adult to be able to help, they must know the whole story, including the blackmail and why you are afraid. As awkward as it is, leaving bits out won't help.

VERBAL

If the **bully** calls you names, insults you, uses put-downs or makes negative or nasty comments about you:

- **Remind yourself** the **bully's** words aren't true. Anyone can say something nasty or negative.

- **Never change** anything about yourself for a **bully**. If you change the way you dress, look or behave, the **bully** will know their words have hurt and they will keep it up.

- **Don't let your brain get tricked.** If you hear the same insults over and over, your brain might try to trick you into believing they are true. They are not. Believing the words will only make you feel bad about yourself.

- **Be proud** of who you are. Never let the **bully** affect the way you think about yourself.

- **Bounce back** nasty words. Try methods in this book or some of your own.

- **Talk** with friends. Tell them what's happening and how you feel. It helps.

BEING EXCLUDED

If the **bully** works by excluding you from things, or trying to make you feel left out or alone:

- **Speak up.** Tell people what's happening and how you feel about it.

- **Never take part.** Ask others in the group to stand up for anyone being **targeted**, including you.

- **Remind yourself** that the **bully** just wants control. The **bully** is wrong, not you.

- **Make good choices**. It can be a tough decision to walk away. If you are only staying because you want to be accepted or are scared to be alone, leaving is the right choice to make.

- **Don't bottle it up**. Talk to people about your choices and ask them to support your decision.

NASTY AND DEMEANING

A bully may want to be ringleader. They may make demeaning or cruel rules that group members have to follow:

- **Never participate** in rituals or follow nasty rules to remain in the group. It could have very bad consequences.

- **Ask yourself**, do you really want to be a part of this group and why?

- **Think** about what healthy friendships are. If the group isn't treating people in a way you would like to be treated, it isn't healthy.

- **Consider** finding others to hang out with. Join new things and look for friends who have values more like yours.

- **Expand** your interests. Try to be involved in different things, and with a variety of people.

- **Respect** yourself and others. Don't compromise your values or behave in a way you know is wrong just to fit in.

RUMOURS AND GOSSIP

If the **bully** works by making things up, sharing your secrets, or spreading rumours and gossip to try to ruin your reputation:

- **Think first** before reacting. You may feel distressed or embarrassed and your first reaction may be to desperately

deny the rumour, or explain which parts aren't true. That's understandable - but not always the best approach.

- **Decide** how damaging the gossip is. If it's nonsense, ignore it. If you believe it may damage you, work out exactly **HOW** it will damage you.

- **Tell** an adult. Speak to trusted adults about what's happening and how you believe it will affect you.

- **Get advice.** Make sure you tell the adult if any part of the gossip is true. Ask them to help you with effective ways to take action.

- **Share** with friends. Tell them what's happening, how you feel and ask for support.

- **Never** pass on nasty rumours. Rumours and gossip can have a big impact on people's lives and self-esteem. Remember that before you pass on something you hear about someone else.

SEXUAL

If the **bully** makes sexual comments, insults, threatens or touches you:

- **Tell them to stop immediately.** If they don't stop, do whatever you can to leave the scene straight away.

- **Don't listen or argue.** If the **bully** tries to blame you or suggest you encouraged their touching or comments, keep moving towards safely.

- **Don't delay.** Don't even **TRY** to sort it out yourself. The most important thing is to make sure it stops straight away. Report it immediately.

- **Don't be embarrassed** or brush it off. Sexual bullying can have really awful consequences. You may not totally understand them all yet, but it is very serious stuff.

And finally, if the bully is a coward who works by using phone, text, email or social media to insult, threaten, share gossip or images, that's called …

CYBERBULLYING

Cyberbullies often say or do cruel things that they would never have the courage to do in person. They may feel less likely to be caught so they feel brave and clever.

Many kids are online every day so cyberbullying can reach a lot of people. It's hard to escape and difficult to stop because it can keep going day and night.

Cyberbullies can be sneaky. There are many dishonest and nasty ways to make a huge impact. Some involve tricking other kids into being involved, or spreading spiteful or wrong information.

So we're not going to talk about the methods cyberbullies use because that could give them ideas they haven't thought of yet. You'll know if you are being cyberbullied without me saying more.

Horrible as cyberbullying is, you can take action. If you don't know how, you **MUST** ask someone with knowledge about devices to help you.

- **Save** the evidence. It's important to keep every text, email, message or photo you see about yourself and make screenshots of websites.

- **Show** an adult what is happening regardless of how embarrassing it is.

- **Never reply** to a **cyberbully**. It will make things worse.

- **Find** the Report Tab. If cyberbullying is happening through a website or social media, report it to the social media group or webmaster.

- **Block** the bullies. Get help to change your privacy settings.

- **Delete** your online account if the bullying gets out of control. As major as that sounds, it may be better than letting it continue.

- **Start a new account** and give the details to trusted people only.

- **Talk** to friends and get their support.

- **Police** may need to be involved if you are afraid or threatened.

If you see cyberbullying, even if it seems harmless, funny or is aimed at someone you don't like, remember ...

- **It is never harmless**. It may look funny or silly to you, but all cyberbullying can do a lot of harm.

- **Never get involved**. Every 'Like' or reply encourages the **bully** and makes things worse.

- **Never share**. If you do, you are helping to spread the nastiness further and have it get more out of control.

- **Try to show support** to the person being bullied. They will be suffering.

- **Let the bully know** you do not approve, but don't do it online. Any participation online can fuel things and make it worse.

Now, there are some things you need to know about ...
SEXTING

Sexting is when someone uses their phone or the internet to send a nude or sexy photo. It's a crime to do this if the photo is of someone under legal age, so that's one big reason not to do it. You could find yourself in lots of trouble, even if you and the person receiving the photo agreed to it.

Some people think sexting is just harmless fun between them and their boyfriend or girlfriend. The problem is, once a photo is sent you can't control what happens to it. And things can go horribly wrong.

Think about what could happen if someone turns nasty and shares your photo with others. The photo can spread from device to device and go viral. Now that can be tough to deal with. Really tough!

It can be humiliating knowing people are looking at sexual photos of you. What makes it worse is that the **bully** is often someone you trusted, like an ex-girlfriend or ex-boyfriend. That means there is also a huge hurt and betrayal to deal with.

When people see these photos they can get totally the wrong idea about the target and the way they behave. They may not want to be friends or worse. Some people have received vulgar, crude or insulting comments about their body and been made fun of. Some have been threatened, harassed or sexually assaulted as a result of the photos. It's serious stuff!

Even when you are older and it's no longer illegal to sext, it's still a really BIG RISK. It's hard to get images off the internet, and impossible to get them off everybody's phones, so don't let them get there in the first place.

There are things you can do so this never happens to you.

- **Delete.** If someone takes a photo of you without your permission, immediately tell them to delete it. If they don't, report them straight away.

- **Keep private things private.** Never let anyone take a sexual photo of you. It might seem like fun at the time but it isn't necessary. Private photos can easily end up in public.

- **Don't be pressured.** If a partner pressures you for a photo, even in a nice way, or takes one without asking, that is a warning sign.

- **Understand** that things change. People meet, hang out and sometimes fall in love, but relationships don't always work out.

- **Remember** you can't predict how someone will behave if a relationship breaks up and things get nasty.

- **Use the 'Family Rule'.** Never share a photo of yourself that you wouldn't share with your family because they and many others may finish up seeing it.

- **Report it** immediately if you see a photo of yourself online or become aware someone is sharing photos.

- **It is a criminal offence to share sexual photos of someone under the legal age.**

So ...

WHERE TO FROM HERE?

Are you going to be part of the **Upstand** against bullying?

If you become an **upstander** you are doing something POSITIVE to stamp out this nasty problem. Start by making a decision never to be a bystander to someone else being bullied. Take it further if you can and try to support others and become an active campaigner against bullying. Get your friends to do the same and stand together. You will feel good about yourself, and you can make a big difference to other people's lives as well. Simply reporting bullying through the right channels so that adults are aware of it can make a huge difference.

And for any bully who is reading this book ...

BULLIES CAN GET HELP TOO

I've spoken about the **bully** as if it's a name, but bullying is not who you are, it's the way you CHOOSE to behave.

If you are bullying someone, deep down you probably aren't really happy about it.

Are you brave enough to ask yourself:

- Why is being popular so important?
- What other ways can I be useful and liked?
- Is bullying really making me feel better about myself?
- Do I like myself more because of it?
- Does bullying really make me feel stronger and less afraid, or is it just a cover up?
- Are the people that admire my bullying really worthwhile friends?

- Does making someone miserable make me feel happier or less alone?

And if you have been bullied or hurt yourself by a child or adult and want payback, trust me, bullying doesn't help. The hurt inside you can't be healed by bullying someone else.

So think about turning it around. Stop bullying, start being nice and:

- **Get respect** instead of fear.
- **Be admired** for what you achieve, not for nasty words or actions.
- **Be liked** instead of followed blindly.
- **Feel good** about yourself.

Bullying has consequences. You could be reported. You could cause lasting damage to someone and that can have dreadful results for them and for you. Do you want to grow up knowing you may be partly responsible if the person you bullied did something foolish or desperate? That will **NEVER** go away.

Some childhood bullies can't kick the habit and continue their bad behaviour as adults. They may **bully** at work, in social situations and at home. They can get into trouble, ruin their own lives, relationships or careers and may meet their match or get a criminal record.

So **STOP**. I know you can and you'll be glad you did. Perhaps you can even try to **UNDO** some of the hurt you caused.

- **Apologise** to people you bullied. It's hard, but it makes you a person to be admired.
- **Admit** you behaved badly. That can be helpful to the people you bullied as well as to you.
- **Tell followers** that you now see that what you are doing is wrong and you are stopping. That can be tough to do, but doing it shows that you are a strong person.

- **Do no more damage.** If you can't apologise, just stop bullying. That's a positive step too.

You made a bad choice to **bully**, but it doesn't have to stay that way. You have many good qualities. Think about that and take the first step to change.

And now to everyone reading this book, I want you to ...

LOOK AFTER YOURSELF

There's a very important thing to remember if you are being bullied.

The bullying will end.

It may be hard to believe but it's true. Being bullied is a horrible thing that is happening now, but it won't last forever. You need to hang in there, take action and get help. One day this will be in the past.

Being bullied is stressful. No one will say it isn't. It can feel like a nightmare in which it is hard to think about anything else. I hope that by feeling empowered you will feel better able to cope if it happens to you.

For some people, the bullying becomes too upsetting and difficult to bear. If you are being bullied and feel:

- Bad about yourself.
- Distressed to the point you can't think clearly.
- Unwell.
- You want to hide away.
- That you just cannot cope.

You **MUST** talk to a parent or trusted adult immediately and tell them **this is serious**.

You need help to manage stress and stay healthy. Make an appointment with a doctor or other professional who can help.

If you are finding it hard to talk about, show the adult this section of the book. By doing that, they will see how badly bullying is affecting you. It's important, as there can be really bad consequences for both yourself and those who love you if you don't seek help for stress if you need it.

Time will move on and you'll grow older and start being with different people. The **bully** will move on too and forget about you because *it was NEVER about you*.

Keep reminding yourself that you have power, there is help available and you can get through. This will end and life will be good again. Remember that and you will be okay.

SO THAT'S ABOUT IT THEN!

There's a lot of information in this book, so go back to different sections, re-read and practice the suggestions. Share what you have learned.

No one deserves to be bullied. No one has the right to be a **bully**. Spread the word that bullying is never okay.

Together we can **upstand** against bullying. Ask anyone who will listen to play a part. Everyone only needs to do a TINY bit, and many people could be saved from the hurt of being bullied.

That's the first step to change.

Be part of it!

Remember, wherever you live, whatever your gender, race, sexuality, culture or religion, you are just as important in this world as everyone else.

Regardless of what you look like, how you dress, your talents or disabilities, whether you are shy, outgoing or somewhere in between, you are a worthwhile person.

If you think a bit differently to people you know or don't always follow the crowd, that's okay! In fact it's more than okay because the world needs people who have fresh, new ideas.

And even if you just blend in without being noticed and don't think you're anyone special, I've got news for you – you are!

Believe in yourself and know that the horrible times will end. Never be afraid to ask for help and always support your friends. Try to be kind to people, and never be deliberately cruel.

Whoever you are, there are things you can do now to help yourself and others. And in your future you will have lots to offer the world. You won't know what yet, so in the meantime be the best person you can and one day you'll find out.

Believe in yourself and that you can help make change. Dare to be different and to speak out. Never let anyone get in the way of your dreams, whatever they may be.

If you can do that, one day you will look back and be proud of all that you have achieved.

Until then, be sure to stay safe and happy.

ABOUT THE AUTHOR

Gina Dawson has qualifications in teaching and counselling and spent fifteen years presenting a range of life-skills programs in schools. Her passions include writing books for children and young adults that promote awareness about personal and social issues, along with short stories. Her prize-winning stories have been published in multiple anthologies and magazines. When not writing the above, Gina assists people to write their memoirs.

Aside from writing, Gina enjoys volunteering for writing and Assistance Dog organisations, dog training, walking, reading, architecture and spending time with family and friends.

We Can Deal With Bullying! is her seventh book.

ABOUT THE ILLUSTRATOR

Kate Bouman is a versatile artist based in east Melbourne who loves to create fun and whimsical images. She works predominantly in digital media and has a particular passion for drawing quirky and characterful animals.

Kate decided to change careers in order to follow her childhood dream of being an illustrator. She completed her Diploma of Illustration in 2018 with awards in portraiture, traditional and digital illustration and lost no time in picking up work, including in book illustration, in which she hopes to advance her career.

Kate has a background in horticulture and enjoys movies, food and city adventuring. *We Can Deal With Bullying!* is her first illustrated children's book.

Other books by Gina Dawson

So That's How I Began!
ISBN: 9781760790233
Modern-day families, body parts, pregnancy and more – this is the book to have on-hand for that moment a child starts asking questions.

So That's What's Happening!
ISBN: 9781760791230
Suitable for boys and girls of any age, this is a warm, all-inclusive introduction to puberty that children will enjoy and parents can relax about.

Next Door's Dog has a Job
ISBN: 9781921024870
Bailey is a very special dog. He is a Service Dog. Join Tom as he discovers exactly what that means, and just how special Bailey is.

Next Door's Dog Goes to School
ISBN: 9781760790523
Grace wants to be able to do everything other children do and now she has Roxie she can. If Grace needs help, Roxie knows exactly what to do.

Next Door's Dog is a Therapy Dog
ISBN: 9781760791360
Leah and Nan are taking Nan's dog Monty to visit people in hospital. Monty makes people laugh, remember and feel comforted. Leah sees that Monty is very special, he is a Therapy Dog.

First published in 2020 by New Holland Publishers
Sydney • Auckland

Level 1, 178 Fox Valley Road, Wahroonga, NSW 2076, Australia
5/39 Woodside Ave, Northcote, Auckland 0627, New Zealand

newhollandpublishers.com

A record of this book is held at the National Library of Australia.

ISBN 9781760791438

Group Managing Director: Fiona Schultz
Publisher: Francesca Roberts-Thomson
Project Editor: Elise James
Designer: Yolanda La Gorcé
Production Director: Arlene Gippert

Printer: Toppan Leefung Printing Ltd

10 9 8 7 6 5 4 3 2 1

Keep up with New Holland Publishers on

 NewHollandPublishers
 @newhollandpublishers

US $14.99

Supporting
New Holland Publishers are extremely proud supporters of the Starlight Children's Foundation and the purchase of this book generates proceeds to further help Starlight…
"Brighten the lives of seriously ill children and their families"
starlight.org.au